Methylene Chloride

U.S. Department of Labor
Elaine L. Chao, Secretary

Occupational Safety and Health Administration
John L. Henshaw, Assistant Secretary

OSHA 3144-06R
2003

I0473860

Contents

Introduction...3

OSHA's Methylene Chloride Standard...3

Exposure Monitoring...5

Medical Surveillance...8

Control Measures...11

Respiratory Protection...13

Hygiene Facilities and Protective
Clothing and Equipment...15

Recordkeeping Requirements...16

Information and Training...17

OSHA Assistance ...18

OSHA Regional Offices...24

Introduction

Methylene chloride and its uses

Methylene chloride, also called dichloromethane, is a volatile, colorless liquid with a chloroform-like odor. Methylene chloride is used in various industrial processes in many different industries: paint stripping, pharmaceutical manufacturing, paint remover manufacturing, metal cleaning and degreasing, adhesives manufacturing and use, polyurethane foam production, film base manufacturing, polycarbonate resin production, and solvent distribution and formulation.

Employee exposure and health consequences

The predominant means of exposure to methylene chloride is inhalation and skin exposure.

OSHA considers methylene chloride to be a potential occupational carcinogen. Short-term exposures to high concentrations may cause mental confusion, lightheadedness, nausea, vomiting, and headache. Continued exposure may also cause eye and respiratory tract irritation. Exposure to methylene chloride may make symptoms of angina more severe. Skin exposure to liquid methylene chloride may cause irritation or chemical burns.

OSHA's Methylene Chloride Standard

Industries covered

The OSHA methylene chloride standard (Title 29 *Code of Federal Regulations*, Parts 1910.1052, 1915.1052, and 1926.1152) covers all occupational exposures to methylene chloride in all workplaces in general industry, shipyard employment, and construction.

Exposure limits

The standard sets a permissible exposure limit (PEL) of 25 parts methylene chloride per million parts of air (ppm) as an eight-hour time-weighted average (TWA). This refers to the average exposure during an eight-hour period. Employers must use engineering and work practice controls to limit employee exposures. Respiratory protection must be used in addition if these controls are insufficient to reduce exposures to below the limits.

The action level for airborne methylene chloride is set at a concentration of 12.5 ppm, calculated as an eight-hour TWA. Reaching or exceeding the action level signals that employers must begin compliance activities such as exposure monitoring and medical surveillance. There is also a short-term exposure limit (STEL) of 125 ppm, as measured over a 15-minute period.

Requirements for regulated areas

The standard requires that the employer establish a regulated area where exposure to airborne concentrations of methylene chloride exceeds or can be expected to exceed either the PEL or the STEL. Employers must mark regulated areas to alert employees to the hazard and minimize the number of authorized employees exposed to methylene chloride.

Employers at multi-employer worksites must notify other employers at the workplace of the locations of all regulated areas and access restrictions. The employer must supply appropriate respiratory protection for each person entering a regulated area. In addition, the employer must ensure that employees wearing respirators do not take medication, chew gum or tobacco, drink, smoke, or apply cosmetics in regulated areas. Nor can employees store any products associated with these activities in a regulated area where the items can become contaminated.

Hazard communication requirements

OSHA's methylene chloride standard requires employers to inform employees that they are working with methylene chloride and to ensure that they understand the hazards associated with exposure to the chemical. Specifically, the rule requires the employer to use labels and material safety data sheets (MSDSs) to let employees know about the health hazards of working with methylene chloride. These include cancer, cardiac effects (including the elevation of carboxyhemoglobin), central nervous system effects, and skin and eye irritation.

These requirements are consistent with those in OSHA's hazard communication standard—29 *CFR* 1910.1200, 29 *CFR* 1915.1200, and 29 *CFR* 1926.59.

Exposure Monitoring

Benefits

Through air sampling and monitoring, employers can better determine methylene chloride exposure, identify the source, and select the proper control methods—resulting in better protection for employees. Exposure monitoring also is key to helping employers determine which other requirements of the standard need to be met.

Measuring employee exposures

To measure an employee's exposure to methylene chloride, the employer must use breathing zone air samples representative of the employee's eight-hour TWA as well as a short-term, 15-minute exposure. To determine eight-hour TWA exposures by representative sampling, employers must take one or more personal breathing zone air samples covering the full-shift exposure for each shift for at least one employee in each job classification in each work area. Employees sampled must be those who are expected to have the highest exposure.

To determine how employee exposures relate to the STEL through representative sampling, employers must take one or more samples covering the highest likely 15-minute exposures associated with those operations for each shift for at least one employee in each job classification in each work area. Employees sampled must be those who are expected to have the highest exposure. When the employer can document comparable exposure levels for similar operations in different work shifts, the employer needs to determine only representative employee exposures for the one shift when the highest exposure is expected.

Initial exposure monitoring

Each employer whose employees are exposed to methylene chloride must perform initial exposure monitoring to accurately determine each affected employee's exposure. However, initial monitoring can be waived when

- Objective data—representing the highest methylene chloride exposure likely to occur during processing, using, or handling—demonstrate that methylene chloride cannot be released in airborne concentrations above the action level or the STEL, or

- Employees are exposed to methylene chloride for fewer than 30 days per year (for example, on a construction site) and the employer uses direct-reading instruments such as a detector tube that gives immediate results, providing enough information to determine what control measures are necessary to reduce exposure to acceptable levels.

Requirements for periodic monitoring

The employer must begin an exposure monitoring program for all tasks where initial monitoring shows that employee exposures are above the action level or STEL. (See Table 1 for monitoring requirements in the standard.) If employee exposure is above the action level, but at or below both the PEL and STEL, employers must monitor employees at least every six months. If exposure is above the PEL or STEL, employers must monitor employees at least every three months. For employees with two consecutive measurements taken at least seven days apart that indicate that exposure has decreased below both the PEL and STEL, employers may change the monitoring schedule from every three months to every six months. When periodic monitoring taken two consecutive times at least seven days apart shows employee exposure is below the action level and the STEL, employers may discontinue monitoring for those employees represented by the monitoring data.

Employers must perform additional monitoring when workplace conditions change—for example, when there is an indication that employee exposures have increased; changes occur in the production process, control equipment, or work practices that could affect exposure levels; and leaks, ruptures, or other breakdowns occur.[1]

[1] Cleanup of methylene chloride spills and repairs to leaks must be made before performing exposure monitoring.

Employers must notify employees of all monitoring results, in writing, either individually or by posting the results in an accessible location, within 15 working days after receipt. When monitoring results show exposures above the PEL or STEL, the notification also must describe the corrective action being taken to reduce exposures to or below these limits.

Employers must allow affected employees or their designated representatives to observe any monitoring. The employer also must provide employees with appropriate protective clothing or equipment needed to enter regulated areas where the monitoring is performed. Employees and their designated representatives must wear the protective clothing and equipment provided and must comply with all other applicable safety and health procedures.

Table 1: Monitoring Requirements

Exposure Scenario	Required Monitoring Activity
Below the action level (12 5 ppm) and at or below the STEL (125 ppm)	No eight-hour TWA or STEL monitoring required
Below the action level (12 5 ppm) and above the STEL (125 ppm)	No eight-hour TWA monitoring required; monitor STEL exposures every three months.
At or above the action level (12.5 ppm), at or below the PEL (25 ppm TWA), and at or below the STEL (125 ppm)	Monitor eight-hour TWA exposures every six months
At or above the action level (12.5 ppm), at or below the PEL (25 ppm TWA), and above the STEL (125 ppm)	Monitor eight-hour TWA exposures every six months and monitor STEL exposures every three months.
Above the PEL (25 ppm TWA), and at or below the STEL (125 ppm)	Monitor eight-hour exposures every three months.
Above the PEL (25 ppm TWA) and above the STEL (125 ppm)	Monitor eight-hour TWA exposures and STEL exposures every three months.

Medical Surveillance

Employer responsibility

Medical surveillance is a comprehensive way to determine if exposure to workplace hazards adversely affects employee health. Frequent, required medical exams or tests can lead to early detection of occupational diseases so preventive measures can be taken to curtail overexposure.

Employers must put a medical surveillance program in place for all employees exposed to methylene chloride. The only exception is when affected employees will be exposed to methylene chloride at or above

- The action level for fewer than 30 days per year, and

- The PEL or STEL for fewer than 10 days during the year.

  Employers also must provide medical surveillance to

- Any employee exposed above the PEL or STEL whom a physician or other licensed health-care professional has identified as being at risk for cardiac disease or some other serious methylene chloride-related health condition and who requests inclusion, regardless of the duration of methylene chloride exposure; and

- All employees during an emergency.

  Employers must provide medical surveillance at no cost to the employee, without loss of pay, and at a reasonable time and place. Medical surveillance must be available

- Before initial work assignment, unless adequate records show an affected employee has received appropriate medical surveillance within the past 12 months.

- Within one year of any initial or subsequent medical surveillance. The frequency of required periodic medical exams varies by age of the employee.[2]

---

[2] Periodic physicals, including appropriate laboratory surveillance, are required as follows: employees 45 years or older—within 12 months of initial or subsequent medical surveillance; employees younger than 45 years—within 36 months of initial or subsequent medical surveillance (unless warranted sooner by a physician or other licensed health-care professional, based on employee's annual medical and work history).

- At the end of employment or reassignment to an area where methylene chloride exposure is consistently below the action level and STEL, if six months or more have elapsed since the last medical surveillance.

- When recommended in the physician's or other licensed health-care professional's[3] written opinion.

For employees working in an atmosphere with methylene chloride concentrations that require them to use a respirator, the examining physician or licensed health-care professional must determine their ability to wear an air-supplied respirator in a negative-pressure mode or a gas mask with an organic vapor canister for emergency escape. The examiner must state this in a written opinion to both the employee and employer.

Requirements for medical surveillance

A physician or licensed health-care professional must perform all medical surveillance procedures. Medical exams[4] must include at least

- A comprehensive medical and work history;[5] and

- A physical exam with special emphasis on the lungs, cardiovascular system including blood pressure and pulse, liver, nervous system, and skin.

The extent of laboratory surveillance[6] is based on the employee's observed health status and medical and work history. The medical surveillance must also include any other information[7] the examining physician or licensed health-care professional determines necessary to provide an appropriate assessment.

[3] A person whose legally permitted scope of practice allows him or her to independently perform the required health-care surveillance activities.
[4] Medical surveillance, such as referrals for consultation or examination, may be provided.
[5] See Appendix B of the standard for an example of the medical and work history format that satisfies this requirement.
[6] See Appendix B of the standard for an example of the methylene chloride standard for medical test recommendations.
[7] When the examining physician or other licensed health-care professional deems it necessary, the scope of the medical exam may be expanded and the appropriate additional medical surveillance provided.

Employers must ensure that medical emergency exams are available in emergency situations and include, at a minimum,

- The appropriate medical treatment and decontamination of the exposed employee;
- A comprehensive physical exam with special emphasis on the nervous system, cardiovascular system including blood pressure and pulse, lungs, liver, and skin;
- An updated medical history as appropriate for the employee's medical condition; and
- Laboratory surveillance as indicated by the employee's health status.

Information for examiners

The employer must provide the examining physician or other licensed health-care professional who is involved in the diagnosis of methylene chloride-induced health effects with

- A copy of the methylene chloride standard and its appendices;
- A description of the affected employee's past, current, and anticipated future duties relating to methylene chloride exposure;
- The employee's former or current methylene chloride exposure levels or anticipated levels, their frequency, and anticipated exposure levels associated with emergencies;
- A description of any personal protective equipment (such as respirators) used or to be used; and
- Information from previous employment-related medical surveillance.

Services employers must arrange

The employer must arrange for the physician or other licensed health-care professional to provide the employer and affected employee a written opinion regarding exam results. This must occur within 15 days of completing the evaluation of the medical and lab findings and not more than 30 days after the exam. The written medical opinion must be limited to

- The physician or licensed health-care professional's opinion whether the employee has any detected medical conditions that would increase the risk of impairment from exposure to methylene chloride;

- Any recommended limitations on employee exposure to methylene chloride and on the use of personal protective clothing or equipment and a respirator;

- A statement that the physician or licensed health-care professional has informed the employee that methylene chloride is a potential carcinogen, of the risk factors for heart disease, and of the potential exacerbation of underlying heart disease from methylene chloride exposure and its metabolism to carbon monoxide; and

- A statement that the physician or licensed health-care professional has informed the employee of medical exam results and any medical conditions resulting from methylene chloride exposure requiring further explanation or treatment.

The examining physician or licensed health-care professional must not reveal to the employer, orally or in writing, any specific records, findings, or diagnoses that have no bearing on occupational exposures to methylene chloride.

Control Measures

How control measures protect employees

Engineering and work practice controls are the primary methods used to reduce workers' exposure to methylene chloride. Employers must use engineering controls and work practices to reduce employee exposure to methylene chloride to or below the PEL and to maintain exposure at these levels. The only exception is when the employer can demonstrate that this is infeasible and that other controls are necessary.

Engineering controls

Examples of engineering controls are local exhaust ventilation, general and special isolation devices, and enclosures.

These controls reduce employee exposure in the workplace by either removing or isolating the hazard or isolating the worker from it. By reducing or removing contaminants from the air, engineering controls reduce or eliminate exposure hazards.

Work practice controls

Work practice controls reduce the likelihood of exposure by altering the way a task is performed. One example is having a worker keep his or her face out of the methylene chloride vapor zone above a dip tank. Another safe practice is to prohibit employees from eating, drinking, smoking, taking medication, or applying cosmetics inside the work area where methylene chloride is used.

Administrative controls

An administrative control removes the worker from exposure. For example, one method of controlling worker exposure to contaminants involves scheduling operations that pose the highest risk of exposure when the fewest employees are present.

However, employee rotation—for example, scheduling several employees to perform work in the exposure area for shorter time limits—is not an effective way to control methylene chloride exposure. That is because, although it may reduce individual exposure, it may increase the number of employees exposed. For this reason, the standard strictly prohibits employee rotation as a means of compliance with the PELs.

Handling methylene chloride leaks

Under the methylene chloride rule, employers must implement procedures to detect methylene chloride leaks. In work areas where spills may occur, provisions must be in place to contain them, clean them up promptly, and dispose of any methylene chloride contaminated waste materials safely. All leaks must be repaired and spills cleaned up by employees who wear appropriate personal protective equipment and are trained in proper cleanup methods.[8]

[9] See Appendix A in the methylene chloride standard for examples of procedures that satisfy this requirement.

Employers covered by this standard also may be covered by the provisions of 29 *CFR* 1910.120(q), Emergency Response to Hazardous Substance Releases.

Respiratory Protection

When respiratory protection is required

Employers must institute engineering, work practice, and administrative controls and maintain their effectiveness to reduce employee exposure to or below the PEL. When this combination of controls does not reduce methylene chloride exposure to or below the PEL and STEL, employers must supplement these controls by providing employees respirators that offer the additional protection.

Respirators protect employees individually by extracting methylene chloride from the air as it is about to be inhaled, or by providing an alternate, non-contaminated source of breathable air. The employer must provide respirators at no cost to each affected employee and ensure their use when

- An employee's exposure to methylene chloride is likely to exceed the PEL and STEL;

- Feasible engineering and work practice controls are being installed or implemented;

- The employer demonstrates that engineering and work practices controls are infeasible, such as in some maintenance operations and repair activities;

- Feasible engineering controls and work practices do not sufficiently reduce exposures to or below the PEL; and

- During emergencies.

More specific requirements are provided in 29 *CFR* 1910.1052(g)(2)(i).

Selecting a respirator

Appropriate respiratory protection varies with exposure levels, as specified in Table 2. Employers must choose atmosphere-supplying respirators from among those approved by the National Institute for

Occupational Safety and Health (NIOSH). Employers may provide NIOSH-approved gas masks with organic vapor canisters, but only for use in emergency escape. The canisters must be replaced after each use before the respirator is returned to service.

Table 2: Minimum Requirements for Respiratory Protection for Airborne Methylene Chloride

Methylene Chloride Airborne Concentration (ppm) or Condition of Use	Minimum Respirator Required*
Up to 625 ppm (25 X PEL)	Continuous flow supplied-air respirator, hood, or helmet
Up to 1,250 ppm (50 X PEL)	(1) Full facepiece supplied-air respirator operated in negative-pressure (demand) mode (2) Full facepiece self-contained breathing apparatus (SCBA) operated in negative-pressure (demand) mode
Up to 5,000 ppm (200 X PEL)	(1) Continuous flow supplied-air respirator, full facepiece (2) Pressure demand supplied-air respirator, full facepiece (3) Positive-pressure full facepiece SCBA
Unknown concentration, or above 5,000 ppm (Greater than 200 X PEL)	(1) Positive-pressure full facepiece SCBA (2) Full facepiece pressure (demand) supplied-air respirator with an auxiliary self-contained air supply
Firefighting	Positive-pressure full facepiece SCBA
Emergency Escape	(1) Any continuous flow or pressure-demand SCBA (2) Gas mask with organic vapor canister

*Respirators assigned for higher airborne concentrations may be used at the lower concentrations.

Where respirators are used, the employer must institute a comprehensive respiratory protection program that complies with 29 *CFR* 1910.134, Respiratory Protection.

Each respirator issued must be fitted properly to ensure the least possible facepiece leakage. For negative-pressure respirators used during emergencies, the employer must perform either qualitative or quantitative fit tests at the initial fitting and then, at least annually. The employer must ensure that employees leave the regulated area to wash their faces and respirator facepieces as necessary to prevent eye or skin irritation associated with respirator use, or if they detect changes in breathing resistance or leakage of the respirator facepiece. If an employee leaves the regulated area because the respirator is malfunctioning, the employer must correct the problem before allowing the employee to return to the regulated area.

Hygiene Facilities and Protective Clothing and Equipment

Hygiene facilities employers must provide

In cases where employees could possibly have skin contact with solutions containing 0.1 percent or more methylene chloride through splashes, spills, or improper work practices, the employer must provide conveniently located washing facilities and ensure that employees use them as needed. Similarly, where there is a potential for eye contact with solutions containing 0.1 percent or more methylene chloride, the employer must provide eyewash facilities within the immediate work area for emergency use and ensure their use when necessary.

Protective clothing and equipment

Employees must use personal protective clothing and equipment where needed to prevent skin or eye irritation due to exposure to methylene chloride. The employer must provide methylene chloride-resistant clothing and equipment at no cost to the employees and ensure that they use it. The employer also must clean, launder, and repair the protective clothing and equipment to keep it effective, and when necessary, replace and dispose of it properly.

Recordkeeping Requirements

Records employers must keep

The employer must establish and keep accurate records for all objective data, exposure monitoring, and medical surveillance in accordance with Access to Employee Exposure and Medical Records, 29 *CFR* 1910.1020. Employee exposure and objective data records must be available for examining and copying by

- Affected employees,
- Former employees,
- Designated employee representatives,
- Anyone who has that employee's written consent,
- The Assistant Secretary of Labor for Occupational Safety and Health, and
- The Director of NIOSH.

Objective data records

If an employer relies on objective data to show that initial monitoring is unnecessary, the record supporting that exemption must include information on

- The methylene chloride-containing material in question;
- The source of the objective data;
- The testing protocol, results, and/or analysis of the material for the release of methylene chloride;
- A description of the exempted operation and how the data support that exemption; and
- Other data relevant to the operations, materials, processing, or employee exposure levels covered by the exemption.

The employer must maintain this record for as long as he or she relies on the objective data.

Exposure measurement records

Employers must keep records of employee exposure measurements for at least 30 years. These records must include the

- Date of measurement for each sample taken;

- Monitored operation involving methylene chloride exposure;

- Sampling and analytical methods used and evidence of their accuracy;

- Number, duration, and results of samples taken;

- Type of personal protective equipment (for example, respirators) worn; and

- Name, social security number, job classification, and exposure monitoring data for all represented employees, indicating which employees were actually monitored.

Medical surveillance records

The employer must keep medical surveillance records for the duration of each affected employee's employment, plus 30 years. These records must include the

- Name and social security number of each affected employee and a description of duties,

- Physician's or other licensed health-care professional's written medical opinions, and

- Employee medical conditions related to methylene chloride exposure.

Information and Training

Information and training employers must provide

The employer must provide information and training to all employees in a manner they understand before or when they are initially assigned to a job in which they could potentially be exposed to methylene chloride. In addition to information required under OSHA's hazard communication standard at 29 *CFR*

1910.1200, 1915.1200, or 1926.59, as appropriate, the employer must inform each affected employee of

- Requirements of the standard, information available in the standard's appendices, and how to access a copy of it in the workplace;

- The quantity, location, manner of use, release, and storage of methylene chloride in cases where exposures could exceed the action level, and the specific nature of operations that could result in such exposure; and

- Where exposures may be above the eight-hour TWA PEL or STEL.

The employer must retrain employees as needed to ensure that each worker exposed at or above the action level or STEL maintains a good understanding of the principles of safe use and handling of methylene chloride in the workplace. Also, when changes in workplace procedures could potentially increase employee exposures so that they might exceed the action level, the employer must update the training to ensure a continued understanding of hazards and control measures. Employers at multi-employer worksites must notify other employers onsite about methylene chloride use in accordance with OSHA's hazard communication standard.

OSHA Assistance

OSHA can provide extensive help through a variety of programs, including assistance about safety and health programs, state plans, workplace consultations, voluntary protection programs, strategic partnerships, alliances, and training and education. An overall commitment to workplace safety and health can add value to your business, to your workplace, and to your life.

Benefits of a safety and health management system

Working in a safe and healthful environment can stimulate innovation and creativity and result in increased performance and higher productivity. The key to a safe and healthful work environment is a comprehensive safety and health management system.

OSHA has electronic compliance assistance tools, or eTools, on its website that walks users through the steps required to develop a comprehensive safety and health program. The eTools are posted at www.osha.gov, and are based on guidelines that identify four general elements critical to a successful safety and health management system:

- Management leadership and employee involvement,
- Worksite analysis,
- Hazard prevention and control, and
- Safety and health training.

State programs

The *Occupational Safety and Health Act of 1970 (OSH Act)* encourages states to develop and operate their own job safety and health plans. OSHA approves and monitors these plans and funds up to 50 percent of each program's operating costs. State plans must provide standards and enforcement programs, as well as voluntary compliance activities, that are at least as effective as federal OSHA's.

Currently, 26 states and territories have their own plans. Twenty-three cover both private and public (state and local government) employees and three states, Connecticut, New Jersey, and New York, cover only the public sector. For more information on state plans, see the list at the end of this publication, or visit OSHA's website at www.osha.gov.

Consultation assistance

Consultation assistance is available on request to employers who want help establishing and maintaining a safe and healthful workplace. Funded largely by OSHA, the service is provided at no cost to small employers and is delivered by state authorities through professional safety and health consultants.

Safety and Health Achievement Recognition Program

Under the consultation program, certain exemplary employers may request participation in OSHA's Safety and Health Achievement Recognition Program (SHARP). Eligibility for participation includes, but is not limited to, receiving a full-service, comprehensive
consultation visit, correcting all identified hazards, and developing an effective safety and health management system.

Employers accepted into SHARP may receive an exemption from programmed inspections (not complaint or accident investigation inspections) for 1 year initially, or 2 years upon renewal. For more information about consultation assistance, visit www.osha.gov

Voluntary Protection Programs

Voluntary Protection Programs (VPP) are designed to recognize outstanding achievements by companies that have developed and implemented effective safety and health management programs. There are three VPP programs: Star, Merit, and Demonstration. All are designed to

- Recognize employers who that have successfully developed and implemented effective and comprehensive safety and health management programs;

- Encourage these employers to continuously improve their safety and health management programs;

- Motivate other employers to achieve excellent safety and health results in the same outstanding way; and

- Establish a cooperative relationship between employers, employees, and OSHA.

VPP participation can bring many benefits to employers and employees, including fewer worker fatalities, injuries, and illnesses; lost-workday case rates generally 50 percent below industry averages; and lower workers' compensation and other injury- and illness-related costs. In addition, many VPP sites report improved employee motivation to work safely, leading to a better quality of life at work; positive community recognition and interaction; further improvement and revitalization of already-good safety and health programs; and a positive relationship with OSHA.

After a site applies for the program, OSHA reviews an employer's VPP application and conducts a VPP onsite evaluation to verify that the site's safety and health management programs are operating effectively. OSHA conducts onsite evaluations on a regular basis.

Sites participating in VPP are not scheduled for regular, programmed inspections. OSHA does, however, handle any employee complaints, serious accidents, or significant chemical releases that may occur at VPP sites according to routine enforcement procedures.

Additional information on VPP is available from OSHA regional offices listed at the end of this booklet and at www.osha.gov.

Cooperative partnerships

OSHA has learned firsthand that voluntary, cooperative partnerships with employers, employees, and unions can be a useful alternative to traditional enforcement and an effective way to reduce worker deaths, injuries, and illnesses. This is especially true when a partnership leads to the development and implementation of a comprehensive workplace safety and health management system.

Alliance program

Alliances enable organizations committed to workplace safety and health to collaborate with OSHA to prevent injuries and illnesses in the workplace. OSHA and its allies work together to reach out to, educate, and lead the nation's employers and their employees in improving and advancing workplace safety and health.

Alliances are open to all, including trade or professional organizations, businesses, labor organizations, educational institutions, and government agencies. In some cases, organizations may be building on existing relationships with OSHA through other cooperative programs.

There are few formal program requirements for alliances, which are less structured than other cooperative agreements, and the agreements do not include an enforcement component. However, OSHA and the participating organizations must define, implement, and meet a set of short- and long-term goals that fall into three categories: training and education; outreach and communication; and promotion of the national dialogue on workplace safety and health.

Strategic Partnership Program

OSHA Strategic Partnerships are agreements among labor, management, and government to improve workplace safety and health. These partnerships encourage, assist, and recognize the efforts of the partners to eliminate serious workplace hazards and achieve a high level of worker safety and health. Whereas OSHA's Consultation Program and VPP entail one-on-one relationships between OSHA and individual worksites, most strategic partnerships build cooperative relationships with groups of employers and employees.

For more information about this program, contact your nearest OSHA office or visit www.osha.gov.

Occupational safety and health training

The OSHA Training Institute in Arlington Heights, Ill., provides basic and advanced training and education in safety and health for federal and state compliance officers, state consultants, other federal agency personnel, and private-sector employers, employees, and their representatives.

Training grants

OSHA awards grants to nonprofit organizations to provide safety and health training and education to employers and workers in the workplace. Grants often focus on high-risk activities or hazards or may help nonprofit organizations in training, education, and outreach.

OSHA expects each grantee to develop a program that addresses a safety and health topic named by OSHA, recruit workers and employers for the training, and conduct the training. Grantees are also expected to follow up with students to find out how they applied the training in their workplaces.

For more information contact OSHA Office of Training and Education, 2020 Arlington Heights Rd., Arlington Heights, IL 60005; or call (847) 297-4810.

Other assistance materials

OSHA has a variety of materials and tools on its website at www.osha.gov. These include eTools such as Expert Advisors and Electronic Compliance Assistance Tools, information on specific health and safety topics, regulations, directives, publications, videos, and other information for employers and employees.

OSHA also has an extensive publications program. For a list of items, visit OSHA's website at www.osha.gov or contact the OSHA Publications Office, U.S. Department of Labor, 200 Constitution Avenue, NW, N-3101, Washington, DC 20210. Telephone (202) 693-1888 or fax to (202) 693-2498.

In addition, OSHA's CD-ROM includes standards, interpretations, directives, and more. It is available for sale from the U.S. Government Printing Office. To order, write to the Superintendent of Documents, U.S. Government Printing Office, Washington, DC 20402, or phone (202) 512-1800.

To contact OSHA

To report an emergency, file a complaint, or seek OSHA advice, assistance, or products, call (800) 321-OSHA or contact your nearest OSHA regional office listed at the end of this publication. The teletypewriter (TTY) number is (877) 889-5627.

Employees can also file a complaint online and get more information on OSHA federal and state programs by visiting OSHA's website at www.osha.gov.

OSHA Regional Offices

Region I
(CT,* ME, MA, NH, RI, VT*)
Boston, MA 02203
(617) 565-9860

Region II
(NJ,* NY,* PR,* VI*)
201 Varick Street, Room 670
New York, NY 10014
(212) 337-2378

Region III
(DE, DC, MD,* PA,* VA,* WV)
The Curtis Center
170 S. Independence Mall West
Suite 740 West
Philadelphia, PA 19106-3309
(215) 861-4900

Region IV
(AL, FL, GA, KY,* MS, NC,* SC,* TN*)
Atlanta Federal Center
61 Forsyth Street SW, Room 6T50
Atlanta, GA 30303
(404) 562-2300

Region V
(IL, IN,* MI,* MN,* OH, WI)
230 South Dearborn Street,
Room 3244
Chicago, IL 60604
(312) 353-2220

Region VI
(AR, LA, NM,* OK, TX)
525 Griffin Street, Room 602
Dallas, TX 75202
(214) 767-4731 or 4736 x224

Region VII
(IA,* KS, MO, NE)
City Center Square
1100 Main Street, Suite 800
Kansas City, MO 64105
(816) 426-5861

Region VIII
(CO, MT, ND, SD, UT,* WY*)
1999 Broadway, Suite 1690
PO Box 46550
Denver, CO 80202-5716
(303) 844-1600

Region IX
(American Samoa, AZ,* CA,* HI, NV,* Northern Mariana Islands)
71 Stevenson Street, Room 420
San Francisco, CA 94105
(415) 975-4310

Region X
(AK,* ID, OR,* WA*)
1111 Third Avenue, Suite 715
Seattle, WA 98101-3212
(206) 553-5930

*These states and territories operate their own OSHA-approved job safety and health programs. (Connecticut, New Jersey, and New York plans cover public employees only.) States with approved programs must have a standard that is identical to, or at least as effective as, the federal standard.

Note: To get contact information for OSHA area offices, OSHA-approved state plans, and OSHA consultation projects, visit www.osha.gov or call (800) 321-OSHA (6742).